Operation Mincemeat: The Ingenious Deception Operation that Changed History

Copyright Page

TITLE: Operation Mincemeat: The Ingenious Deception Operation that Changed History

1ST Edition

ISBN: 9798223251804

Table of Contents

Operation Mincemeat: The Ingenious Deception Operation that Changed History

By Roberto Miguel Rodriguez

Chapter 1: The Origins of Operation Mincemeat

The Need for Deception in World War II

World War II was a time of immense conflict and strategic maneuvering, where victory often hinged on the ability to deceive the enemy and gain a tactical advantage. Operation Mincemeat, one of the most ingenious deceptions in history, exemplified the crucial role that deception played in the war effort. This subchapter will delve into the necessity of deception during World War II, focusing specifically on the various aspects of Operation Mincemeat.

In the realm of military history, Operation Mincemeat stands out as a remarkable example of tactical deception. By planting false documents on a corpse and letting it wash ashore in enemy territory, the British were able to mislead the Germans into believing that their next target was Sardinia, rather than the actual objective, Sicily. The meticulous planning and attention to detail involved in this operation underscore the importance of deception as a military strategy.

Espionage and intelligence gathering were integral components of Operation Mincemeat. The covert operations and intelligence techniques employed by the British were crucial in obtaining the necessary information to execute the deception successfully. By infiltrating enemy intelligence networks and manipulating the flow of information, the British were able to create a believable narrative that fooled even the most astute German intelligence officers.

Psychological warfare played a significant role in Operation Mincemeat. The psychological impact of discovering the false documents on the corpse, coupled with the manipulation tactics employed by the British, instilled doubt and confusion in the minds of the German high command. This psychological advantage was instrumental in diverting German resources away from the true target and ultimately changing the course of the war.

Operation Mincemeat was not an isolated incident but rather part of a broader strategy of deception employed by various countries during World War II. Studying other deceptive operations carried out during the war provides valuable insights into the tactics and techniques employed in Operation Mincemeat.

The Royal Navy played a crucial role in executing Operation Mincemeat. Their expertise in naval operations and their ability to transport the corpse to the intended destination were essential to the success of the deception. Understanding the naval component of Operation Mincemeat sheds light on the logistical challenges involved and the coordination required to execute such a complex operation.

Codebreaking and cryptography were also pivotal in deciphering enemy communications, allowing the British to intercept and interpret vital information related to Operation Mincemeat. The role of codebreaking in this deception operation highlights the significance of intelligence gathering and analysis in strategic planning.

Operation Mincemeat had a profound historical significance and impacted the outcome of World War II. Investigating the historical implications of this operation provides valuable insights into the overall war effort and the strategies employed by the Allied forces.

The intelligence analysis leading up to Operation Mincemeat was a meticulous process that involved gathering, analyzing, and interpreting information from various sources. Understanding the intelligence analysis process provides a comprehensive perspective on the decision-making and strategic planning involved in executing deceptive operations.

Finally, studying the propaganda and misinformation campaigns employed in Operation Mincemeat sheds light on the use of psychological manipulation and the implications of propaganda in war. The British were able to exploit the power of misinformation to mislead and confuse the enemy, further emphasizing the need for deception during World War II.

In conclusion, Operation Mincemeat exemplifies the need for deception in World War II. By exploring the intricacies of this operation within the niches of military history, espionage and intelligence, psychological warfare, deception operations, naval operations, codebreaking, strategic planning, historical investigations, intelligence analysis, and propaganda, historians can gain a comprehensive understanding of the impact and significance of this ingenious deception that changed the course of history.

The Birth of Operation Mincemeat

Operation Mincemeat, one of the most ingenious deceptions in the history of warfare, was conceived and executed by the British during World War II. This subchapter delves into the birth of this operation, exploring its origins, planning, and execution. Addressed to historians and enthusiasts of military history, espionage, and intelligence, this subchapter provides a comprehensive overview of Operation Mincemeat and its various facets.

Operation Mincemeat began its journey in 1943, when the British intelligence agency, MI6, sought to deceive the Axis powers and divert their attention away from the impending Allied invasion of Sicily. The idea was hatched by Lieutenant Commander Ewen Montagu and approved by Admiral John Godfrey. They devised a plan to plant false information on a corpse, which would be washed ashore in enemy territory, leading the Axis forces to believe that the Allies planned to attack Greece instead of Sicily.

The key to the success of Operation Mincemeat lay in the meticulous planning and attention to detail. A suitable body was obtained from a deceased homeless man and transformed into a fictional character named Major William Martin. The corpse was dressed in an officer's uniform, equipped with fake documents, and given a personal history to lend credibility to the deception. A briefcase containing false letters from high-ranking British officials was handcuffed to the body, further enhancing the illusion.

The Royal Navy played a pivotal role in executing Operation Mincemeat. The submarine HMS Seraph was chosen to transport the body to the Spanish coastline, where it would be discovered by German agents. The submarine crew faced numerous challenges during the journey, including rough seas and the risk of being detected by German patrols. However, their determination and skill ensured the safe delivery of the corpse to the designated location.

The success of Operation Mincemeat lay not only in the physical execution but also in the psychological impact it had on the Axis powers. The deception planted seeds of doubt and confusion among the German intelligence community, diverting their attention away from the true target. The operation showcased the power of psychological warfare and manipulation tactics employed by the British intelligence agencies.

This subchapter also explores the larger context of Operation Mincemeat within the framework of World War II. It examines other deception operations carried out by various countries during the war and highlights the significance of Operation Mincemeat in the overall strategic planning. The role of codebreaking and cryptography in deciphering enemy communications and its relevance to Operation Mincemeat is also investigated.

As historians, it is crucial to delve into the historical investigations surrounding Operation Mincemeat and analyze its impact on the outcome of World War II. Furthermore, this subchapter delves into intelligence analysis, propaganda, and misinformation campaigns employed in Operation Mincemeat, shedding light on their implications and long-term effects.

In conclusion, the birth of Operation Mincemeat marked a turning point in the history of deception operations during World War II. This subchapter provides historians with a detailed account of the planning, execution, and impact of this ingenious deception. From military tactics to espionage techniques, psychological warfare to codebreaking, Operation Mincemeat encompassed a wide range of disciplines, making it a fascinating subject for historians and enthusiasts alike.

Selecting the Target: The Strategic Importance of Operation Mincemeat

Operation Mincemeat, the ingenious deception that changed history, holds a significant place in the annals of World War II. This subchapter delves into the strategic importance of selecting the target for this audacious operation, which had far-reaching implications for the outcome of the war. Historians, with a keen interest in military history, espionage and intelligence, psychological warfare, deception operations during World War II, naval operations, codebreaking and cryptography, strategic planning, historical investigations, intelligence analysis, and propaganda and misinformation, will find this exploration particularly enlightening.

The selection of the target for Operation Mincemeat was a meticulous process that required careful analysis and consideration. The primary objective was to deceive the Axis powers, specifically the German high command, into believing that the Allied forces would launch an attack on Greece rather than Sicily. The strategic implications of this deception were immense, as it diverted crucial German resources away from the actual target, allowing the Allies to secure a significant advantage in the Mediterranean theater.

This subchapter will examine the intelligence gathering, analysis, and interpretation process that led to the selection of Sicily as the decoy target. It will delve into the codebreaking and cryptography efforts employed to decipher enemy communications, which played a pivotal role in identifying Sicily as a key German objective. The coordination and strategic planning involved in executing Operation Mincemeat will also be explored, shedding light on the intricate details and tactics employed by the Royal Navy.

In addition, this subchapter will analyze the psychological impact of Operation Mincemeat and the manipulation tactics employed to ensure its success. It will delve into the use of propaganda and misinformation campaigns, investigating their implications and the broader context of psychological warfare during World War II. The historical significance of Operation Mincemeat and its lasting impact on the outcome of the war will be thoroughly examined, providing historians with a comprehensive understanding of this groundbreaking deception operation.

Ultimately, the strategic importance of selecting the target for Operation Mincemeat cannot be overstated. This subchapter aims to provide historians with a detailed account of the intelligence, planning, and psychological warfare involved in this operation. By studying the intricacies of Operation Mincemeat, historians can gain valuable insights into the art of deception, the complexities of military strategy, and the enduring impact of covert operations in shaping the course of history.

The Planning and Coordination Process

Operation Mincemeat: The Ingenious Deception That Changed History

In the annals of World War II, few operations have captured the imagination and strategic brilliance as Operation Mincemeat. This audacious British deception operation, carried out in 1943, played a pivotal role in the outcome of the war. The planning and coordination process behind this operation was nothing short of remarkable, involving meticulous attention to detail, tactical acumen, and psychological warfare strategies.

The success of Operation Mincemeat hinged on the collaboration and coordination of various branches of the British military and intelligence services. It was a multidimensional endeavor that required the expertise of naval officers, codebreakers, intelligence analysts, and strategic planners. Each component played a crucial role in ensuring the seamless execution of this audacious deception.

At the heart of the planning process was the creation of a fictitious identity for a deceased British officer, "Major William Martin." This involved the fabrication of a detailed backstory, complete with personal letters, identification documents, and even love letters. The level of attention to detail was extraordinary, with every aspect meticulously designed to deceive the enemy.

Codebreaking and cryptography played a pivotal role in the planning and coordination of Operation Mincemeat. The deciphering of enemy communications enabled the British to identify potential vulnerabilities and exploit them to their advantage. The information gleaned from intercepted messages allowed the planners to tailor their deception to exploit German weaknesses and divert their attention away from the actual Allied invasion plans.

Psychological warfare tactics were also employed during the planning and coordination process. The planners understood the power of misinformation and propaganda in manipulating the enemy's perception. By strategically leaking false information, they were able to create confusion and sow doubt within the German high command.

Strategic planning and coordination were the cornerstones of Operation Mincemeat. Every aspect of the operation was carefully orchestrated, from the selection of the body to the timing of the deception. The planners meticulously analyzed every potential risk and accounted for contingencies, ensuring that the operation would unfold seamlessly.

Operation Mincemeat stands as a testament to the ingenuity, resourcefulness, and strategic brilliance of the British military and intelligence services. It exemplifies the power of deception, intelligence analysis, and psychological warfare in shaping the course of history. The planning and coordination process behind this operation remains a fascinating case study for historians, intelligence analysts, and military strategists alike, offering valuable insights into the complexities of World War II deception operations and the lasting impact they had on the outcome of the war.

Chapter 2: The Execution of Operation Mincemeat

Naval Operations: The Royal Navy's Role

During World War II, the Royal Navy played a crucial role in executing Operation Mincemeat, an ingenious deception that changed the course of history. This subchapter delves into the naval operations involved in this covert mission, shedding light on the strategic planning, coordination, and execution that took place at sea.

Operation Mincemeat aimed to deceive the Axis powers, particularly the German military, by planting false information to mislead their intelligence gathering efforts. The success of this operation relied heavily on the involvement of the Royal Navy, which played a pivotal role in ensuring the smooth execution of the deception.

One key aspect of naval operations in Operation Mincemeat was the transportation of the fabricated documents and the body of a fictitious British officer, Major William Martin. The Royal Navy was responsible for delivering these critical elements to the coast of Spain, where they would be discovered by the enemy. The coordination and planning required to safely transport such sensitive material across hostile waters demonstrated the Navy's expertise in covert operations.

Furthermore, the Royal Navy provided crucial support in terms of naval intelligence and codebreaking. The Navy's codebreakers, working closely with the famed Bletchley Park codebreaking team, deciphered enemy communications, allowing for a deeper understanding of the German naval operations and ensuring that the deception remained convincing.

Additionally, the Royal Navy played a significant role in protecting the operation from detection. Naval vessels patrolled the waters, ensuring that German patrols or submarines did not intercept the operation or compromise its secrecy. This naval presence was essential in maintaining the integrity of the mission and preventing any leaks that could have jeopardized its success.

The successful execution of Operation Mincemeat was a testament to the Royal Navy's expertise in strategic planning, coordination, and intelligence gathering. Their contributions were instrumental in the overall success of the operation, which had far-reaching implications for the outcome of World War II.

For historians interested in naval operations during World War II, the Royal Navy's role in Operation Mincemeat offers a fascinating insight into the complexities of deception operations at sea. By examining the specific tactics and strategies employed by the Navy, historians can gain a deeper understanding of the challenges faced and the impact of naval operations on the outcome of the war.

In conclusion, the Royal Navy's involvement in Operation Mincemeat was indispensable to the success of this groundbreaking deception operation. This subchapter aims to provide historians with a comprehensive analysis of the naval operations and their significance in executing Operation

Mincemeat, highlighting the critical role played by the Royal Navy in shaping the outcome of World War II.

Codebreaking and Cryptography: Deciphering Enemy Communications

During World War II, one of the most crucial elements of intelligence gathering and covert operations was the ability to decipher enemy communications. The use of codes and ciphers by the Axis powers presented a significant challenge for the Allies, who relied on intercepting and decoding these messages to gain valuable information about enemy plans and intentions. Nowhere is this more evident than in the remarkable story of Operation Mincemeat, a British deception operation that changed the course of history.

Operation Mincemeat, carried out in 1943, required meticulous planning, coordination, and, most importantly, the ability to break enemy codes. The operation involved the creation of a fictitious officer, Major William Martin, who carried false documents outlining plans for an invasion of Greece. These documents, planted on a dead body, were meant to mislead the German forces into believing that the Allies were planning an attack on Greece instead of Sicily.

To ensure the success of Operation Mincemeat, the British intelligence agencies, particularly the Government Code and Cypher School, played a crucial role. The codebreakers at Bletchley Park, including renowned mathematician Alan Turing, worked tirelessly to decrypt German and Italian codes, allowing the planners of Mincemeat to anticipate enemy responses and tailor their deception accordingly.

The success of codebreaking in deciphering enemy communications was not limited to Operation Mincemeat. It played a pivotal role in many other deceptive operations carried out during World War II. The ability to intercept and decode enemy messages allowed the Allies to gather vital intelligence, disrupt enemy plans, and mislead their adversaries.

The role of codebreaking and cryptography in Operation Mincemeat highlights the importance of intelligence gathering and analysis in military operations. The ability to understand and interpret enemy communications provided the Allies with a significant advantage, allowing them to strategically plan and execute successful deception operations.

Moreover, the use of codebreaking and cryptography in Operation Mincemeat also demonstrates the psychological impact and manipulation tactics employed in wartime. By deceiving the German forces and diverting their attention away from the true target, the Allies were able to exploit the enemy's fears, biases, and vulnerabilities.

The story of Operation Mincemeat is a testament to the power of intelligence, strategic planning, and psychological warfare during World War II. It showcases the ingenuity and resourcefulness of the British intelligence agencies and their role in shaping the outcome of the war. The successful deciphering of enemy communications through codebreaking and cryptography was a critical factor in the triumph of Operation

Mincemeat and serves as a compelling case study for historians, military strategists, and intelligence analysts alike.

Strategic Planning: Coordinating the Deception Operation

In the annals of military history, Operation Mincemeat stands as a testament to the power of strategic planning and coordination. This ingenious deception operation, executed during World War II, not only changed history but also showcased the immense capabilities of the British intelligence and military apparatus.

At its core, Operation Mincemeat aimed to deceive the Axis powers, specifically Nazi Germany, about the Allied invasion plans in the Mediterranean. To achieve this, a meticulous plan was crafted that involved the coordination of various elements, including espionage, intelligence gathering, psychological warfare, and naval operations.

The strategic planning for Operation Mincemeat began with the selection of a suitable target: the Mediterranean theater. The planners recognized the strategic importance of this region and understood that diverting German attention from an invasion there would greatly benefit the Allied cause.

To execute this deception, a deceased British officer, Major William Martin, was carefully chosen as the protagonist of the operation. His body was equipped with false documents, including letters and a personal diary, which convincingly indicated plans for an Allied invasion of Greece and Sardinia.

The success of Operation Mincemeat hinged on the meticulous attention to detail and the flawless execution of the plan. To ensure the believability of the deception, the planners meticulously researched the personal details of Major Martin, ensuring they aligned with his purported mission. The letters and documents were carefully crafted to deceive even the most astute German intelligence officers.

The Royal Navy played a vital role in the execution of Operation Mincemeat. They ensured the safe delivery of Major Martin's body to the Spanish coast, where it was discovered by German agents. The Navy's coordination with British intelligence agencies and the strategic use of naval resources demonstrated the effectiveness of joint operations in achieving military objectives.

Moreover, the role of codebreaking and cryptography cannot be overstated in the success of Operation Mincemeat. The deciphering of enemy communications allowed British intelligence to gain invaluable insights into German operations and tailor their deception accordingly. The intelligence analysis leading up to the operation was a testament to the meticulousness and dedication of the codebreakers and intelligence officers involved.

Operation Mincemeat holds historical significance not only for its immediate impact on the outcome of World War II but also for its lasting influence on subsequent military operations. The operation showcased the power of psychological warfare, propaganda, and misinformation campaigns, which continue to be employed in modern-day conflicts.

In conclusion, the strategic planning and coordination involved in Operation Mincemeat exemplify the ingenuity and effectiveness of British intelligence and military operations during World War II. The operation's success, achieved through meticulous attention to detail, coordination with naval forces, codebreaking, and psychological manipulation, has left an indelible mark on military history and continues to captivate historians and specialists in espionage, intelligence, and strategic planning.

Intelligence Analysis: Gathering, Analyzing, and Interpreting Information

Intelligence analysis is a crucial aspect of any military operation, and it played a pivotal role in the success of Operation Mincemeat during World War II. This subchapter delves into the intricate process of gathering, analyzing, and interpreting information that led to the ingenious deception that changed history.

Operation Mincemeat was a British deception operation carried out in 1943 with the goal of misleading the Axis powers regarding the location of the Allied invasion of Sicily. In order to execute this audacious plan, a deceased body was planted off the coast of Spain, carrying false documents that suggested an impending Allied attack in Greece instead of Sicily.

The intelligence gathering process for Operation Mincemeat was meticulous and multi-faceted. Analysts scoured various sources, including intercepted enemy communications, human intelligence reports, and aerial reconnaissance, to gather as much information as possible. The challenge was to identify the most reliable and relevant pieces of information amidst a sea of data.

Once the information was gathered, it underwent a rigorous analysis process. Analysts examined the credibility of the sources, cross-referenced different pieces of information, and identified patterns and inconsistencies. This analysis allowed them to separate the important details from the noise and to gain a deeper understanding of enemy intentions and capabilities.

Interpreting the information was a delicate task. Analysts had to consider the larger strategic context, assess the potential impact of the deception operation, and anticipate the enemy's likely response. This required a deep understanding of the enemy's psychology, as well as the ability to think strategically and creatively.

Operation Mincemeat also involved the use of psychological warfare and manipulation tactics. Through the deliberate planting of false information, the British sought to exploit the enemy's fears, biases, and preconceptions. This subchapter explores the psychological impact of such operations and the implications of using deception as a strategic tool.

Understanding the intelligence analysis process behind Operation Mincemeat provides historians with valuable insights into the intricate workings of covert operations during World War II. It sheds light on the role of intelligence gathering and analysis in shaping military strategies, as well as the importance of psychological warfare and the use of deception to gain the upper hand in conflicts.

By studying Operation Mincemeat, historians can gain a deeper understanding of the broader historical context, the impact of intelligence analysis on the outcome of World War II, and the relevance of deception operations in shaping military tactics. This subchapter serves as a comprehensive exploration of the intelligence analysis process leading up to Operation Mincemeat and its historical significance.

Psychological Warfare: Manipulation Tactics and their Impact

In the annals of military history, there are few operations as ingenious and impactful as Operation Mincemeat. This covert World War II British deception operation employed a variety of manipulation tactics that not only deceived the enemy but also had a profound psychological impact on the course of the war.

At its core, Operation Mincemeat was a psychological warfare campaign designed to manipulate the enemy's perception of British military intentions. By planting false information on a corpse, the British intended to deceive the Axis powers regarding their plans for the invasion of Sicily. This manipulation tactic, known as the "Mincemeat ruse," relied on the enemy's willingness to believe the information presented to them, ultimately diverting their attention and resources away from the true objective.

The psychological impact of Operation Mincemeat cannot be overstated. It created a sense of confusion and uncertainty among the enemy ranks, sowing doubt and mistrust in their decision-making processes. The success of the operation relied on the enemy's psychological vulnerability, exploiting their fears and preconceived notions about British military strategies. This manipulation of the enemy's mindset played a crucial role in the ultimate success of the invasion of Sicily.

Furthermore, Operation Mincemeat showcased the power of deception operations during World War II. It was just one example of the many creative and strategic deceptions employed by various countries during the war. By studying Operation Mincemeat, historians can gain valuable insights into the intricacies of deceptive practices and their impact on the outcome of the conflict.

The Royal Navy played a pivotal role in executing Operation Mincemeat. Their expertise in naval operations, combined with their understanding of the psychological impact of deception, was instrumental in carrying out this elaborate ruse. The coordination and strategic planning involved in the operation demonstrated the importance of meticulous preparation and execution in achieving success.

Codebreaking and cryptography also played a significant role in Operation Mincemeat. The intelligence gathered through these methods provided crucial insights into enemy communications, allowing the British to tailor their deception tactics accordingly. This highlights the relevance of codebreaking in shaping the outcome of the operation and the war as a whole.

As historians delve into the historical significance of Operation Mincemeat, they uncover its profound impact on the outcome of World War II. By analyzing the intelligence gathering, analysis, and interpretation process leading up to the operation, historians can gain a deeper understanding of the complexities involved in intelligence analysis and its implications for military strategies.

Finally, Operation Mincemeat also sheds light on the use of propaganda and misinformation campaigns during the war. The British employed these tactics to amplify the psychological impact of the operation, further manipulating the enemy's perception of reality. This aspect of the operation underscores the power of propaganda in shaping public opinion and military strategies.

In conclusion, Operation Mincemeat stands as a testament to the power of psychological warfare and manipulation tactics. Its impact on the outcome of World War II cannot be overstated. By studying this operation, historians gain valuable insights into the details, tactics, and psychological impact of deception operations, making it a compelling subject for those interested in military history, espionage and intelligence, psychological warfare, and the broader context of World War II.

Chapter 3: Espionage and Intelligence Techniques in Operation Mincemeat

Covert Operations: The Art of Deception

Operation Mincemeat: The Ingenious Deception That Changed History

In the annals of military history, there are few operations as audacious and effective as Operation Mincemeat. This covert operation, carried out by the British during World War II, employed a sophisticated web of deception, intelligence gathering, and psychological warfare to deceive the enemy and alter the course of the war. This subchapter delves into the intricate details and tactics employed during Operation Mincemeat, shedding light on its historical significance and impact on the outcome of the war.

At its core, Operation Mincemeat was an elaborate ruse that aimed to deceive the Axis powers regarding the Allied invasion plans. The operation involved planting a dead body, equipped with false identity documents and misleading intelligence, off the coast of Spain. This body, purportedly that of a British officer, carried documents indicating an imminent Allied attack in Sardinia and Greece, diverting German attention away from the true target, Sicily.

The success of Operation Mincemeat relied heavily on espionage and intelligence gathering techniques. British intelligence operatives meticulously crafted a persona for the deceased officer, Major William Martin, ensuring his background and personal details aligned with the false narrative. They also utilized codebreaking and cryptography to intercept and decipher enemy communications, gaining crucial insights into their plans and mindset.

Psychological warfare played a pivotal role in Operation Mincemeat. The British employed manipulation tactics to exploit the psychological vulnerabilities of the Axis powers, sowing doubt, confusion, and paranoia among their ranks. By strategically disseminating false information and carefully orchestrating the discovery of Major Martin's body, they played on the fears and insecurities of the enemy, altering their perception of the impending Allied invasion.

Operation Mincemeat was not an isolated incident in the realm of deception operations during World War II. This subchapter also explores other deceptive operations carried out by different countries during the war, drawing parallels and highlighting the unique aspects of Operation Mincemeat. It delves into the role of the Royal Navy in executing the operation, the strategic planning and coordination involved, and the intelligence analysis and interpretation process leading up to its implementation.

Furthermore, this subchapter delves into the historical investigations surrounding Operation Mincemeat, analyzing its impact on the outcome of World War II. It investigates the relevance of codebreaking and cryptography in deciphering enemy communications and the use of propaganda and misinformation campaigns, shedding light on the broader implications of such tactics.

For historians fascinated by military history, espionage, intelligence, psychological warfare, deception operations, naval operations, codebreaking, strategic planning, historical investigations, intelligence analysis, and propaganda, this subchapter provides a comprehensive exploration of Operation Mincemeat. It reveals the artistry and ingenuity behind this extraordinary covert operation that forever changed the course of history.

Intelligence Gathering: Infiltrating Enemy Networks

Operation Mincemeat: The Ingenious Deception That Changed History

In the annals of military history, few operations have been as masterfully executed as Operation Mincemeat during World War II. This covert operation, carried out by the British, not only demonstrated the power of espionage and intelligence gathering but also showcased the art of psychological warfare and deception.

At the heart of Operation Mincemeat lay the audacious plan to deceive the Axis powers by planting false information. The goal was to mislead the enemy about the location of the Allied invasion of Southern Europe, ultimately diverting German troops and resources away from the intended target. To achieve this, intelligence operatives embarked on a daring mission to infiltrate enemy networks and manipulate their understanding of the situation.

The success of Operation Mincemeat hinged on the careful gathering of intelligence. British intelligence agencies meticulously scoured enemy communications, intercepting and deciphering coded messages to gain invaluable insights into German military operations and strategies. This information formed the foundation of the deception plan, providing crucial details that could be exploited to maximum effect.

However, intelligence gathering alone was not enough. The psychological impact of Operation Mincemeat was equally significant. By planting false documents and personal effects on a deceased body that was intentionally left adrift off the coast of Spain, the British aimed to convince the Germans that the Allies were planning an invasion of Greece instead of Sicily. The manipulation of enemy perceptions through carefully crafted misinformation campaigns played a pivotal role in the success of this operation.

The Royal Navy played a crucial role in executing Operation Mincemeat, providing the means to deliver the planted documents and ensuring the deception appeared genuine. The coordination and strategic planning involved in this operation were extraordinary, involving multiple agencies and meticulous attention to detail. The operation showcased the importance of effective collaboration in achieving military objectives.

Operation Mincemeat was not an isolated event; it was part of a broader context of deception operations during World War II. By studying various deceptive operations carried out by different countries, historians can gain a deeper understanding of the complexities and impact of psychological warfare during the conflict.

Moreover, Operation Mincemeat highlighted the significance of codebreaking and cryptography in deciphering enemy communications. The role of intelligence analysis cannot be overstated, as it involved the meticulous gathering, analysis, and interpretation of information leading up to the operation. The use of propaganda and misinformation campaigns in Operation Mincemeat further emphasizes the power of psychological manipulation in warfare.

In conclusion, Operation Mincemeat stands as a testament to the ingenuity and audacity of intelligence gathering and deception operations during World War II. The careful infiltration of enemy networks, the strategic planning, and the psychological impact of the operation all played a crucial role in changing the course of history. By delving into the details and tactics of Operation Mincemeat, historians can uncover valuable insights into the art of espionage, intelligence gathering, and psychological warfare during this critical period.

Misinformation Campaigns: Propaganda and Disinformation

Operation Mincemeat, the ingenious deception that changed history, involved a complex web of propaganda and disinformation campaigns. This subchapter delves into the role of misinformation in the success of this World War II British deception operation, exploring its implications and impact on various niches such as military history, espionage, psychological warfare, deception operations during the war, naval operations, codebreaking, strategic planning, historical investigations, and intelligence analysis.

Propaganda played a crucial role in Operation Mincemeat, as the British sought to deceive the Axis powers about their true intentions. By creating a false identity for a deceased British officer, the Allies aimed to mislead the Germans into believing that an attack on Greece was imminent, diverting their attention from the true target: Sicily. The meticulous planning and execution of this misinformation campaign showcased the creative brilliance and strategic thinking of the British intelligence agencies.

The subchapter explores the covert operations and intelligence gathering techniques employed in Operation Mincemeat. It delves into the psychological impact of the operation, analyzing the manipulation tactics employed to deceive the enemy and the broader implications for psychological warfare during World War II. The study of deception operations carried out by different countries during the war, including Operation Mincemeat, offers valuable insights into the evolving nature of warfare and intelligence strategies.

Naval operations also played a significant role in executing Operation Mincemeat, as the Royal Navy had to ensure the successful delivery of the false information to the enemy. The subchapter investigates the role of the Royal Navy and examines the challenges they faced in executing this mission.

Furthermore, the subchapter delves into the relevance of codebreaking and cryptography in deciphering enemy communications, highlighting their importance in Operation Mincemeat and the broader context of World War II intelligence operations. It explores how the intelligence gathering, analysis, and interpretation process led to the successful execution of this deception operation.

The strategic planning and coordination involved in Operation Mincemeat are also explored, shedding light on the meticulous preparation and execution required for such a complex operation. By investigating the historical significance of Operation Mincemeat, historians can gain a deeper understanding of its impact on the outcome of World War II.

In conclusion, this subchapter provides a comprehensive analysis of the use of propaganda and misinformation campaigns in Operation Mincemeat and their implications. It offers valuable insights for historians, military enthusiasts, intelligence analysts, and anyone interested in understanding the intricacies of this remarkable deception operation.

Codebreaking and Cryptography: Breaking the Enemy's Secrets

During World War II, codebreaking and cryptography played a crucial role in deciphering enemy communications and gaining valuable intelligence. One of the most notable examples of this was Operation Mincemeat, a British deception operation that had a significant impact on the outcome of the war. This subchapter will delve into the role of codebreaking in Operation Mincemeat and its relevance to the larger picture of the war.

Codebreaking was a complex and intricate process that involved deciphering encrypted messages sent by the enemy. The British codebreakers at Bletchley Park, led by Alan Turing, were at the forefront of this effort. Their expertise in breaking the German Enigma machine codes was instrumental in gathering crucial intelligence. However, Operation Mincemeat introduced a new challenge for the codebreakers – the need to maintain secrecy and not compromise the operation.

In order to deceive the Germans, the British employed a variety of codes and ciphers to ensure that the enemy would not suspect the authenticity of the information they were receiving. These codes were carefully crafted to mimic the style and language used by the Germans, making it difficult for the codebreakers to distinguish between genuine and false information.

The success of Operation Mincemeat relied heavily on the codebreakers' ability to decipher and analyze these codes. By intercepting and decrypting enemy communications, the British were able to gather valuable intelligence about German military plans and intentions. This information was then strategically used to mislead and manipulate the enemy, creating a psychological impact that played a crucial role in the overall success of the operation.

The subchapter will explore the various methods and techniques employed by the British codebreakers, as well as the challenges they faced in deciphering the enemy's secrets. It will also delve into the collaboration between the codebreakers and the other branches of the military, particularly the Royal Navy, in executing Operation Mincemeat.

Additionally, the subchapter will provide a broader perspective on the role of codebreaking and cryptography in World War II. It will examine other deceptive operations carried out by different countries, highlighting the importance of intelligence gathering and analysis in military strategy.

Overall, this subchapter will offer historians and enthusiasts of military history, espionage, intelligence, and psychological warfare a detailed insight into the significance of codebreaking and cryptography in Operation Mincemeat, as well as its broader relevance in the context of World War II.

Chapter 4: The Psychological Impact of Operation Mincemeat

Understanding Psychological Warfare

Psychological warfare is a tactic that has been employed throughout history to manipulate and influence the thoughts, emotions, and behaviors of individuals and groups. In the context of Operation Mincemeat, a World War II British deception operation, psychological warfare played a crucial role in shaping the outcome of the war.

The objective of Operation Mincemeat was to deceive the Axis powers, specifically Germany, into believing that the Allies would launch an attack on Greece instead of Sicily. By strategically planting false information and creating an elaborate ruse, the British aimed to divert German resources away from the actual target and gain a strategic advantage.

Psychological warfare was essential in executing this deception. The operation involved the use of a deceased body, disguised as a British officer, and carefully crafted documents that suggested an impending Allied invasion of Greece. The psychological impact of discovering the body and the credibility of the documents were crucial in convincing the Germans of the authenticity of the operation.

Understanding the psychological impact and manipulation tactics employed in Operation Mincemeat offers valuable insights into the effectiveness of psychological warfare. The operation relied on exploiting cognitive biases, such as confirmation bias and the tendency to believe information that aligns with preconceived notions. By presenting the Germans with information that supported their existing beliefs and expectations, the British were able to manipulate their decision-making processes.

Furthermore, Operation Mincemeat utilized propaganda and misinformation campaigns to reinforce the credibility of the deception. The British carefully disseminated false information to German intelligence sources, ensuring that the ruse appeared legitimate from multiple angles. This manipulation of information and the subsequent psychological impact on the German decision-makers highlights the intricacies of psychological warfare.

Studying psychological warfare within the context of Operation Mincemeat provides historians with a deeper understanding of the complexities involved in covert operations during World War II. It also sheds light on the role of intelligence gathering, analysis, and interpretation in executing successful deception operations. By analyzing the tactics employed in Operation Mincemeat, historians can gain insights into the broader strategies and techniques employed by different countries during the war.

In conclusion, psychological warfare played a crucial role in Operation Mincemeat, a deception operation that had a significant impact on the outcome of World War II. By understanding the psychological impact and manipulation tactics employed in this operation, historians can gain valuable insights into the complexities of covert operations, intelligence analysis, and the broader historical significance of psychological warfare during the war.

Manipulation Tactics: Exploiting Cognitive Biases

In the fascinating world of espionage and deception, Operation Mincemeat stands out as a shining example of psychological warfare and manipulation tactics employed during World War II. This subchapter delves into the intricacies of how cognitive biases were cleverly exploited to achieve the desired outcomes.

Operation Mincemeat, a British deception operation executed in 1943, aimed to deceive the Axis powers about the Allied intentions for the invasion of Sicily. The success of this operation hinged upon the meticulous understanding and exploitation of cognitive biases that influence human decision-making.

One such cognitive bias that played a crucial role in Operation Mincemeat was the Confirmation Bias. The planners behind the operation carefully crafted a false identity for a deceased British officer, complete with forged documents and personal effects. By presenting information that aligned with the Axis powers' preconceived notions of Allied intentions, they effectively reinforced their existing beliefs, thus increasing the likelihood of the deception being accepted as genuine.

Another cognitive bias exploited in Operation Mincemeat was the Authority Bias. The planners understood that individuals tend to trust and accept information from authoritative sources without questioning it. To capitalize on this bias, they strategically planted false information in the form of confidential documents, which were designed to appear as if they had been leaked from high-ranking military officials. This manipulation technique aimed to lend credibility to the overall deception and increase the chances of it being perceived as reliable intelligence.

Additionally, the planners leveraged the Bandwagon Effect, exploiting the tendency of individuals to adopt beliefs or behaviors simply because they seem popular or widely accepted. They carefully disseminated false information through various channels, including intercepted enemy communications and strategically placed informants. By creating an illusion of consensus among the enemy ranks, they aimed to sway their decision-making processes and divert their attention away from the true Allied intentions.

Operation Mincemeat serves as a remarkable case study in the art of psychological warfare and manipulation tactics. By skillfully exploiting cognitive biases such as Confirmation Bias, Authority Bias, and the Bandwagon Effect, the planners behind this operation achieved a stunning deception that changed the course of history. This subchapter invites historians and enthusiasts of military history, espionage and intelligence, psychological warfare, and deception operations during World War II to explore the intricacies of Operation Mincemeat and its lasting impact. Through a comprehensive analysis of the manipulation tactics employed, readers will gain a deeper understanding of the power of cognitive biases in shaping human perception and decision-making processes, both on and off the battlefield.

Historical Investigations: Unraveling the Psychological Impact

In the realm of military history, there are few operations as intriguing and impactful as Operation Mincemeat. This covert deception mission, carried out by the British during World War II, forever altered the course of history. However, what often goes overlooked is the psychological impact that this audacious scheme had on both the enemy and the Allies.

Operation Mincemeat was not simply a matter of executing a tactical plan; it was a carefully orchestrated psychological warfare campaign. The goal was to deceive the enemy into believing that the Allies planned to invade Greece instead of Sicily, thus diverting German resources away from the true target.

To achieve this, the British employed a wide range of manipulation tactics. They meticulously crafted a false identity for a deceased officer, complete with fabricated personal documents and letters. These documents were designed to convince the enemy that the invasion of Greece was imminent and that the officer held vital information about the operation.

The psychological impact of Operation Mincemeat cannot be overstated. The German High Command fell for the ruse hook, line, and sinker. They diverted troops and resources to Greece, leaving the real invasion force in Sicily largely unopposed. This strategic victory had a profound impact on the outcome of the war.

To fully understand the historical significance of Operation Mincemeat, it is essential to investigate the psychological warfare techniques employed. The meticulous planning and execution of this operation serve as a case study in the effectiveness of deception operations during World War II.

Furthermore, the psychological impact of Operation Mincemeat sheds light on the importance of intelligence analysis and codebreaking. The success of the operation relied on the British accurately interpreting enemy communications and exploiting their vulnerabilities.

By studying the psychological impact of Operation Mincemeat, historians gain valuable insights into the strategic planning and coordination necessary for such a complex operation. Additionally, it offers a unique perspective on the role of naval operations and the Royal Navy's involvement in executing the mission.

The use of propaganda and misinformation campaigns in Operation Mincemeat further deepens our understanding of the broader context of World War II. It highlights the power of psychological warfare and the implications it has on shaping the course of history.

In conclusion, the subchapter "Historical Investigations: Unraveling the Psychological Impact" delves into the fascinating realm of Operation Mincemeat. By exploring the psychological impact and manipulation tactics employed in this audacious deception operation, historians can gain a deeper understanding of its historical significance and its impact on the outcome of World War II.

Propaganda and Misinformation: Shaping Public Opinion

In the realm of military operations, the use of propaganda and misinformation has long been recognized as a powerful tool for shaping public opinion. Operation Mincemeat, the ingenious deception that changed history during World War II, provides a fascinating case study in the strategic use of propaganda and misinformation to achieve military objectives.

At its core, Operation Mincemeat was a covert operation carried out by the British intelligence agency, MI5, and the Royal Navy in 1943. The operation aimed to deceive the Axis powers into believing that the Allies planned to invade Greece instead of Sicily, the actual target. To achieve this, the British employed a combination of psychological warfare, deception tactics, and misinformation campaigns.

One of the key elements of Operation Mincemeat was the creation of a false identity for a deceased British officer, Major William Martin. This involved planting false documents on the body of a deceased man, carefully chosen to appear as if he had died in a plane crash while carrying top-secret documents outlining plans for an invasion of Greece. These documents were meticulously crafted to mislead the enemy, presenting a false narrative that would shape their perception of the Allies' intentions.

The success of Operation Mincemeat relied heavily on the manipulation of public opinion through propaganda. The British intelligence agencies strategically leaked false information to the Axis powers through their intelligence networks, ensuring that the misinformation reached the right channels. This deliberate dissemination of false information created confusion and uncertainty among the enemy, diverting their attention and resources away from the actual target.

The use of propaganda and misinformation in Operation Mincemeat highlights the importance of psychological warfare in military operations. By exploiting the enemy's cognitive biases and preconceptions, the British were able to exploit the power of perception and shape the narrative surrounding their military intentions.

From a historical perspective, Operation Mincemeat stands as a significant example of the effectiveness of propaganda and misinformation in achieving strategic military objectives. It paved the way for future deception operations during World War II and beyond, highlighting the enduring relevance of psychological warfare in modern military conflicts.

For historians, Operation Mincemeat offers a rich tapestry of espionage, intelligence gathering, codebreaking, and strategic planning. It serves as a case study in the intricate coordination and execution of a complex deception operation. Furthermore, it underscores the critical role of intelligence analysis in deciphering enemy communications and drawing meaningful insights from fragmented information.

In conclusion, the use of propaganda and misinformation in Operation Mincemeat played a pivotal role in shaping public opinion and achieving strategic military objectives. By studying this fascinating historical event, historians can gain valuable insights into the intricacies of psychological warfare, intelligence analysis, and the broader impact of deception operations during World War II.

Chapter 5: Deception Operations During World War II

The Use of Deception in Modern Warfare

In the subchapter titled "The Use of Deception in Modern Warfare," we delve into the fascinating world of Operation Mincemeat, a World War II British deception operation that forever changed the course of history. This chapter is specifically addressed to historians and enthusiasts interested in various aspects of Operation Mincemeat, such as military history, espionage and intelligence, psychological warfare, deception operations during World War II, naval operations, codebreaking and cryptography, strategic planning, historical investigations, intelligence analysis, and propaganda and misinformation.

Operation Mincemeat stands as a testament to the power of deception in the realm of warfare. It was an audacious plan that involved creating a fictional identity for a dead body, complete with falsified documents, to deceive the enemy. The aim of this operation was to mislead the German forces and divert their attention away from the true target of the Allied invasion of Sicily.

This chapter explores the intricate details and tactics employed in Operation Mincemeat, shedding light on the covert operations and intelligence gathering techniques that were instrumental in its success. From the careful selection of the deceased body to the creation of a believable backstory, every aspect of this operation was meticulously planned and executed.

Moreover, we delve into the psychological impact and manipulation tactics employed in Operation Mincemeat. The operation relied heavily on exploiting the enemy's expectations and preconceived notions, playing on their fears and desires to create a believable narrative. By understanding the psychology of their adversaries, the British forces were able to manipulate their perceptions and actions to their advantage.

We also examine the broader context of deception operations during World War II, drawing comparisons between Operation Mincemeat and other deceptive operations carried out by different countries during the war. By studying these operations, we gain valuable insights into the evolving strategies and techniques employed by nations to gain an upper hand in warfare.

Furthermore, we explore the role of the Royal Navy in executing Operation Mincemeat, highlighting the importance of naval operations in the success of this deception. The chapter also touches upon the role of codebreaking and cryptography in deciphering enemy communications and its relevance to Operation Mincemeat, showcasing the crucial role of intelligence in planning and executing such operations.

Lastly, we investigate the historical significance of Operation Mincemeat and its impact on the outcome of World War II. By analyzing the intelligence gathering, analysis, and interpretation process leading up to Operation Mincemeat, we gain a deeper understanding of the complex web of information that contributed to its success. Additionally, we study the use of propaganda and misinformation campaigns in Operation

Mincemeat and their implications, highlighting the power of psychological warfare and the manipulation of information in modern warfare.

In conclusion, the subchapter "The Use of Deception in Modern Warfare" provides historians and enthusiasts with a comprehensive exploration of Operation Mincemeat, shedding light on the intricacies of this ingenious deception operation. By studying the details, tactics, and psychological impact of Operation Mincemeat, readers gain valuable insights into the role of deception in warfare, its historical significance, and its impact on the outcome of World War II.

Notable Deceptive Operations by Various Countries

Throughout the course of World War II, numerous countries engaged in deceptive operations to gain an advantage over their adversaries. One of the most notable of these operations was Operation Mincemeat, a British deception operation that had a significant impact on the outcome of the war. However, it is important to recognize that Operation Mincemeat was not an isolated incident. Several other countries also employed deceptive tactics to mislead their enemies and achieve their military objectives.

One such example is the German operation known as Operation Greif. Led by the infamous SS officer Otto Skorzeny, Operation Greif aimed to infiltrate enemy lines by using captured American tanks and vehicles. German soldiers dressed as American soldiers, spoke fluent English, and carried forged identification documents. This deception allowed them to confuse and disrupt

Allied forces, creating chaos and exploiting vulnerabilities in their defense.

Another notable deceptive operation was the Soviet Union's Operation Zeppelin. This operation involved the creation of a fictitious military unit, complete with fabricated orders, radio transmissions, and troop movements. The goal was to deceive German intelligence and divert attention away from the actual Soviet offensive. By creating a false threat, the Soviet Union was able to catch the Germans off guard and gain a tactical advantage.

Similarly, the United States employed deception tactics in their Pacific campaign against Japan. Operation Vengeance, for example, was a successful mission to assassinate Admiral Isoroku Yamamoto, the architect of the Pearl Harbor attack. The Americans used decrypted Japanese communications to pinpoint Yamamoto's location and then launched a surprise attack, effectively deceiving the Japanese and avenging the devastating attack on Pearl Harbor.

These examples demonstrate the widespread use of deception during World War II by various countries. Operation Mincemeat, however, stands out as a particularly ingenious and effective operation. By planting false documents on a deceased body and allowing it to wash ashore, the British were able to deceive the German intelligence and divert their attention away from the actual Allied invasion plans. This deception played a crucial role in the success of the D-Day landings and ultimately changed the course of history.

Studying these various deceptive operations provides valuable insights into the intricacies of military strategy, intelligence gathering, and psychological warfare during World War II. It highlights the importance of strategic planning, coordination, and the use of misinformation and propaganda to achieve military objectives. Operation Mincemeat, along with other notable deceptive operations, continues to captivate historians and shed light on the complex nature of warfare and the power of deception.

Operation Mincemeat: A Case Study in Deception

Operation Mincemeat, also known as the "Man Who Never Was," is a remarkable example of deception during World War II. This covert operation, executed by the British intelligence agency MI5, played a pivotal role in shaping the outcome of the war. In this subchapter, we delve into the details and tactics employed in Operation Mincemeat, examining its historical significance, impact on the war, and the various disciplines involved.

Military history enthusiasts will find a treasure trove of information in this subchapter. We explore the intricate planning and coordination required to execute such a complex operation. From the strategic placement of a deceased body with falsified documents to the crafting of an elaborate backstory, every detail was meticulously designed to deceive the enemy.

Espionage and intelligence aficionados will be fascinated by the covert operations and intelligence gathering techniques employed in Operation Mincemeat. The subchapter delves into the world of spies, codebreakers, and cryptography, revealing the vital role they played in deciphering enemy communications. We analyze the intelligence gathering, analysis, and interpretation process leading up to Operation Mincemeat, shedding light on the intricate web of information that was pieced together.

Psychological warfare experts will find a deep analysis of the psychological impact and manipulation tactics employed in Operation Mincemeat. We explore how the British intelligence agency exploited the enemy's fears and desires, using propaganda and misinformation campaigns to deceive and manipulate their thinking. The subchapter also highlights the implications of these psychological tactics and their broader implications in the context of war.

For historians interested in the broader context of World War II, this subchapter provides a comprehensive study of deception operations carried out by various countries during the war. By comparing and contrasting Operation Mincemeat with other deceptive operations, we gain a deeper understanding of the strategies employed by different nations and the impact they had on the outcome of the war.

Naval operations enthusiasts will be particularly interested in the role of the Royal Navy in executing Operation Mincemeat. This subchapter examines the challenges faced by the naval forces, their strategic planning, and the crucial role they played in ensuring the success of the operation.

Codebreaking and cryptography enthusiasts will appreciate the exploration of how codebreaking played a vital role in deciphering enemy communications, revealing the relevance of this discipline to Operation Mincemeat. We delve into the challenges faced by codebreakers and the significance of their contributions to the success of the operation.

Finally, historians and intelligence analysts will find this subchapter invaluable in investigating the historical significance of Operation Mincemeat. We explore its impact on the outcome of World War II and analyze the intelligence analysis process leading up to the operation. By studying the use of propaganda and misinformation campaigns, we gain insights into the broader implications of these tactics in the context of war.

In conclusion, "Operation Mincemeat: A Case Study in Deception" is a subchapter that offers an in-depth exploration of the various disciplines involved in this ingenious deception operation. From military history to espionage, from psychological warfare to naval operations, this subchapter provides a comprehensive study of Operation Mincemeat and its historical significance.

Chapter 6: Historical Significance of Operation Mincemeat

Impact on the Outcome of World War II

Operation Mincemeat, the clever and audacious British deception operation during World War II, played a significant role in shaping the outcome of the war. This subchapter examines the impact of Operation Mincemeat on various aspects of the conflict, highlighting its influence on military history, espionage and intelligence, psychological warfare, deception operations, naval operations, codebreaking and cryptography, strategic planning, historical investigations, intelligence analysis, and the use of propaganda and misinformation.

From a military history perspective, Operation Mincemeat stands out as a prime example of meticulous planning and execution. The operation's success relied on the careful coordination of various military branches, including the Royal Navy, which played a crucial role in transporting the false information. By studying the details and tactics employed in Operation Mincemeat, historians gain valuable insights into the complexities of wartime operations.

Espionage and intelligence enthusiasts will find Operation Mincemeat particularly fascinating. This operation exemplifies the use of covert operations and intelligence gathering techniques to deceive the enemy. The ingenious manipulation of enemy intelligence channels allowed the British to mislead the Axis powers and divert their attention away from their intended targets. The subchapter delves into the methods employed, providing a comprehensive analysis of the intelligence gathering, analysis, and interpretation process leading up to Operation Mincemeat.

Psychological warfare played a crucial role in Operation Mincemeat. The operation relied heavily on psychological impact and manipulation tactics to deceive the enemy. By analyzing these aspects, historians gain a deeper understanding of the psychological dynamics at play during wartime and the effectiveness of such tactics.

Operation Mincemeat was not an isolated incident during World War II. Deceptive operations were carried out by various countries, each with their own objectives and strategies. By studying Operation Mincemeat in the context of other deception operations, historians can assess the effectiveness and significance of this particular operation.

The impact of Operation Mincemeat extends beyond military operations. The use of codebreaking and cryptography was instrumental in deciphering enemy communications and analyzing intelligence. This subchapter explores the role of codebreaking in relation to Operation Mincemeat, shedding light on the crucial role of cryptography in wartime intelligence.

Furthermore, the strategic planning and coordination required for Operation Mincemeat were immense. This subchapter examines the strategic planning process and the coordination efforts involved, providing valuable insights into the complexities of wartime decision-making.

Historical investigations into Operation Mincemeat reveal its profound significance. The operation not only influenced the outcome of World War II but also shaped the course of history. By examining its historical significance, historians can fully appreciate the impact of Operation Mincemeat on the war and its lasting implications.

Finally, the subchapter explores the use of propaganda and misinformation campaigns in Operation Mincemeat. The operation employed these tactics to mislead and deceive the enemy. By studying the implications of propaganda and misinformation, historians gain a deeper understanding of the role of information warfare in World War II and its impact on the outcome of the conflict.

In conclusion, Operation Mincemeat had a profound impact on the outcome of World War II. By examining its influence on military history, espionage and intelligence, psychological warfare, deception operations, naval operations, codebreaking and cryptography, strategic planning, historical investigations, intelligence analysis, and propaganda and misinformation, historians gain a comprehensive understanding of this ingenious deception operation and its significance in shaping the course of history.

Lessons Learned: Influence on Future Deception Operations

Operation Mincemeat, the ingenious deception that changed history, offers invaluable lessons that have significantly influenced future deception operations. This subchapter explores the impact of Operation Mincemeat on various aspects of military history, espionage and intelligence, psychological warfare, deception operations during World War II, naval operations, codebreaking and cryptography, strategic planning, historical investigations, intelligence analysis, and propaganda and misinformation campaigns.

In the realm of military history, Operation Mincemeat stands as a remarkable example of the intricate details and tactics employed during World War II. Historians can delve into the meticulous planning and execution of this operation to understand the level of sophistication and innovation achieved by the British forces.

Espionage and intelligence enthusiasts can explore the covert operations and intelligence gathering techniques utilized in Operation Mincemeat. The operation showcased the effectiveness of using fabricated intelligence to deceive the enemy and gain a strategic advantage. It serves as a case study for understanding the intricacies of intelligence operations during wartime.

Psychological warfare analysts can analyze the psychological impact and manipulation tactics employed in Operation Mincemeat. The operation utilized the power of deception to manipulate the enemy's perception, causing them to divert resources and make critical mistakes. The study of these tactics can provide valuable insights into the psychological aspects of warfare and its influence on decision-making.

Deception operations during World War II are a crucial area of study, and Operation Mincemeat holds a prominent place within this realm. By examining various deceptive operations carried out by different countries during the war, historians can gain a comprehensive understanding of the strategies employed and their impact on the outcome of battles and campaigns.

The role of the Royal Navy in executing Operation Mincemeat is another aspect that deserves exploration. Naval operations played a significant role in the success of the operation, and understanding the intricacies of their involvement can provide insights into the coordination required between different branches of the military.

Codebreaking and cryptography enthusiasts can investigate the role of codebreaking in deciphering enemy communications, particularly its relevance to Operation Mincemeat. The operation's success heavily relied on the ability to intercept and interpret enemy messages accurately.

Strategic planning and coordination were critical elements in the execution of Operation Mincemeat. By examining the strategic planning involved, historians can gain insights into the level of detail required for successful deception operations.

Historical investigations into Operation Mincemeat shed light on its significance and impact on the outcome of World War II. By analyzing its consequences, historians can identify how this deception operation shaped the course of history.

Intelligence analysis enthusiasts can delve into the intelligence gathering, analysis, and interpretation process leading up to Operation Mincemeat. This investigation can provide valuable insights into the methodology and techniques employed in gathering and analyzing intelligence during wartime.

Finally, the study of propaganda and misinformation campaigns in Operation Mincemeat offers a unique perspective on the use of these tactics in warfare. The operation's success hinged on the successful dissemination of false information, highlighting the power of propaganda and its implications in military operations.

In conclusion, Operation Mincemeat has left an indelible mark on various niches, including military history, espionage and intelligence, psychological warfare, deception operations, naval operations, codebreaking and cryptography, strategic planning, historical investigations, intelligence analysis, and propaganda and misinformation campaigns. Its lessons continue to shape and influence future deception operations, making it an essential topic for historians and enthusiasts alike.

Legacy and Historical Interpretations

Operation Mincemeat: The Ingenious Deception That Changed History

Introduction:

Operation Mincemeat was a remarkable World War II British deception operation that had a profound impact on the outcome of the war. This subchapter explores the legacy and historical interpretations of this audacious operation, examining its significance, impact, and the various techniques employed. It delves into the broader context of deception operations during the war, the role of the Royal Navy, codebreaking, strategic planning, intelligence analysis, and the use of propaganda and misinformation.

Historical Significance:

Operation Mincemeat played a pivotal role in the Allied victory during World War II. By convincing the Axis powers that the Allies were planning to invade Greece rather than Sicily, it diverted crucial German resources and allowed the successful Allied invasion of Sicily in 1943. This operation not only demonstrated the effectiveness of deception tactics but also showcased the ingenuity and audacity of British intelligence.

Covert Operations and Intelligence Gathering Techniques:

Operation Mincemeat involved an intricate network of spies, agents, and intelligence officers. This subchapter delves into the covert operations and intelligence gathering techniques employed, including the use of double agents, forged documents, and the manipulation of enemy communications. It explores how these techniques were utilized to deceive the enemy and gain a strategic advantage.

Psychological Warfare and Manipulation Tactics:

The success of Operation Mincemeat relied heavily on psychological warfare and manipulation tactics. By exploiting the enemy's fears, desires, and expectations, British intelligence created a convincing narrative that the Axis powers fell for. This subchapter analyzes the psychological impact of the operation on both the enemy and the Allies and delves into the manipulation tactics employed to ensure its success.

Strategic Planning and Coordination:

Operation Mincemeat required meticulous strategic planning and coordination. This subchapter explores the complexities involved in executing such a large-scale deception operation, including the selection of the target, the creation of a credible backstory, and the coordination between various intelligence agencies and military branches. It highlights the role of the Royal Navy in executing the operation and the challenges they faced.

Codebreaking and Cryptography:

Codebreaking played a crucial role in deciphering enemy communications and gathering intelligence leading up to Operation Mincemeat. This subchapter investigates the role of codebreaking in the operation, emphasizing its relevance and significance in ensuring the success of the deception. It delves into the codebreaking techniques employed and the impact they had on the operation's execution.

Historical Investigations and Intelligence Analysis:

The historical investigations surrounding Operation Mincemeat have shed light on its significance and impact on the outcome of World War II. This subchapter explores the various interpretations and analyses carried out by historians, intelligence experts, and military strategists. It examines the intelligence gathering, analysis, and interpretation process leading up to the operation, highlighting the lessons learned and the contributions made by those involved.

Propaganda and Misinformation Campaigns:

The use of propaganda and misinformation campaigns was a key aspect of Operation Mincemeat. This subchapter studies the role of propaganda in shaping public opinion and influencing the enemy's perception. It analyzes the implications of using propaganda and misinformation in a military deception operation, exploring its ethical considerations and the impact it had on the success of Operation Mincemeat.

Conclusion:

Operation Mincemeat stands as one of the most audacious and successful deception operations of World War II. Its legacy and historical interpretations continue to captivate historians and specialists in military history, espionage, intelligence, psychological warfare, naval operations, codebreaking, strategic planning, historical investigations, intelligence analysis, and propaganda. By studying this operation, we gain valuable insights into the art of deception and its impact on the course of history.

Chapter 7: Conclusion

Recapitulation of the Key Findings

In this subchapter, we will provide a comprehensive recapitulation of the key findings discussed throughout the book "Operation Mincemeat: The Ingenious Deception That Changed History." Addressed to historians and enthusiasts of Operation Mincemeat, the 1943 World War II British deception operation, this section aims to summarize the most crucial discoveries and shed light on the significance of this covert mission.

First and foremost, Operation Mincemeat was a meticulously planned deception operation carried out by the British intelligence agency MI5 during World War II. The objective was to deceive the Axis powers, particularly the German high command, about the Allied invasion plans in Europe. The operation involved the use of a deceased individual, known as "Major William Martin," whose body was dressed as a Royal Marine officer and dropped off the coast of Spain, along with fabricated documents suggesting an imminent Allied attack on Greece and Sardinia.

One of the key findings of this book reveals the immense success of Operation Mincemeat. The false information provided by the planted documents was believed by the Germans, diverting their attention away from the actual target - Sicily. As a result, the subsequent Allied invasion of Sicily, codenamed Operation

Husky, encountered significantly less resistance and became a pivotal turning point in the war.

Furthermore, the book delves into the intricate details of the planning and execution of Operation Mincemeat. It uncovers the individuals involved, such as Lieutenant Commander Ewen Montagu and his team, and their relentless efforts to create a credible cover story for the deceased Major Martin. By meticulously crafting a fake identity, including personal letters, photographs, and even a love affair, the team ensured that the deception would be convincing enough to fool the enemy intelligence.

Another significant finding explores the ethical and moral implications of Operation Mincemeat. The book examines the ethical dilemmas faced by those involved in the operation, particularly the decision to use a deceased body for deception purposes. It offers a thought-provoking analysis of the justifiability of such actions during times of war and the consequential impact on the course of history.

In conclusion, the recapitulation of the key findings from "Operation Mincemeat: The Ingenious Deception That Changed History" highlights the remarkable success and intricacies of this covert operation. By diverting German attention and altering the course of the war, Operation Mincemeat played a pivotal role in the Allied victory. Furthermore, the book provides valuable insights into the planning, execution, and ethical considerations surrounding this historical event. For historians and enthusiasts of World War II deception operations, this subchapter offers a concise summary of the significant findings explored throughout the book.

Evaluation of Operation Mincemeat's Historical Significance

Operation Mincemeat, the ingenious deception operation conducted by the British during World War II, holds immense historical significance. This subchapter aims to delve into the various aspects of Operation Mincemeat and its impact on the outcome of the war, focusing on the niches of military history, espionage and intelligence, psychological warfare, deception operations, naval operations, codebreaking and cryptography, strategic planning, historical investigations, intelligence analysis, and propaganda and misinformation.

In terms of military history, Operation Mincemeat stands out for its intricate details and tactics. The operation involved planting false documents on a deceased body, which was then intentionally left to wash ashore in enemy territory. This deception successfully misled the Axis powers, diverting their attention from the true target of the Allied invasion. The meticulous planning, coordination, and execution of the operation highlight the strategic brilliance of the British military.

Espionage and intelligence were at the heart of Operation Mincemeat. The covert operations and intelligence gathering techniques employed in this operation demonstrated the extent to which intelligence agencies could manipulate the enemy's perception and decision-making processes. By feeding false information to the Axis powers, the British effectively undermined their strategic planning and disrupted their operations.

Operation Mincemeat also had a profound psychological impact. The manipulation tactics employed, such as using personal letters and creating a fictional identity for the deceased body, played on the emotions and vulnerabilities of the enemy. This psychological warfare had far-reaching implications, as it weakened the morale of the Axis powers and sowed doubt and confusion among their ranks.

When examining deception operations during World War II, Operation Mincemeat is a prime example of the ingenuity and effectiveness of such tactics. The operation showcased the power of misdirection and misinformation in warfare, highlighting the importance of strategic deception in achieving military objectives.

Naval operations played a crucial role in executing Operation Mincemeat. The Royal Navy's involvement in transporting the body and ensuring its discovery in enemy territory was instrumental in the success of the operation. This highlights the significance of naval forces in supporting and facilitating covert operations during the war.

Codebreaking and cryptography were also relevant to Operation Mincemeat. The decryption of enemy communications played a pivotal role in identifying vulnerabilities and formulating effective deception strategies. This emphasizes the importance of intelligence analysis and the role of codebreaking in warfare.

Operation Mincemeat's historical significance can be further explored through the lens of strategic planning. The meticulous planning and coordination required to execute such a complex operation underscore the importance of strategic foresight and attention to detail in achieving military objectives.

Historical investigations into Operation Mincemeat reveal its impact on the outcome of World War II. The diversion of the Axis powers' resources and attention towards the false target directly contributed to the success of the Allied invasion. The operation's historical significance lies in its ability to alter the course of the war and shape its outcome.

Intelligence analysis is a critical aspect of Operation Mincemeat. The gathering, analysis, and interpretation of intelligence played a crucial role in formulating the deception strategy. This underscores the importance of intelligence agencies in supporting military operations and achieving strategic objectives.

Finally, the use of propaganda and misinformation campaigns in Operation Mincemeat highlights the power of psychological manipulation in warfare. By disseminating false information, the British were able to influence the enemy's perception and decision-making processes, further emphasizing the significance of psychological warfare in achieving military success.

In conclusion, Operation Mincemeat's historical significance is multifaceted and far-reaching. Its impact on military history, espionage and intelligence, psychological warfare, deception operations, naval operations, codebreaking and cryptography, strategic planning, historical investigations, intelligence analysis, and propaganda and misinformation campaigns make it a pivotal event in World War II. By evaluating these aspects, historians can gain a comprehensive understanding of the operation's historical significance and its implications for the outcome of the war.

Implications for Future Historical Investigations

As historians delve into the fascinating story of Operation Mincemeat, they are confronted with a multitude of implications that extend far beyond the immediate scope of this ingenious deception. This subchapter aims to shed light on the various implications for future historical investigations, providing a framework for further exploration and analysis.

One of the key implications lies in the realm of military history. Operation Mincemeat, a crucial World War II British deception operation, offers a unique opportunity to focus on the details and tactics employed during this period. Historians can dissect the intricate planning and execution of this operation, studying its impact on the overall war effort and the lessons that can be learned from it.

Furthermore, Operation Mincemeat provides a rich case study for espionage and intelligence enthusiasts. The covert operations and intelligence gathering techniques employed in this operation offer valuable insights into the world of espionage. Historians can analyze the methodologies used, explore the role of intelligence agencies, and assess the effectiveness of these techniques in achieving strategic objectives.

From a psychological warfare perspective, Operation Mincemeat presents a captivating analysis of the psychological impact and manipulation tactics employed during wartime. Historians can delve into the intricacies of psychological warfare, studying the methods used to deceive the enemy and manipulate their perceptions. This subchapter offers a unique opportunity to explore the psychological dimensions of war and their implications on military strategies.

Moreover, Operation Mincemeat forms part of a broader context of deception operations during World War II. By studying various deceptive operations carried out by different countries, historians can gain a comprehensive understanding of the strategies employed during this period. Operation Mincemeat serves as a valuable case study within this larger framework, shedding light on the intricacies of wartime deception.

The role of the Royal Navy in executing Operation Mincemeat is another aspect that warrants historical investigation. By examining the naval operations involved in this operation, historians can gain insights into the coordination, planning, and execution of naval strategies during World War II. This subchapter serves as a springboard for further exploration into the naval aspects of Operation Mincemeat.

Codebreaking and cryptography also played a significant role in deciphering enemy communications during World War II. By investigating the role of codebreaking in relation to Operation Mincemeat, historians can deepen their understanding of the relevance of codebreaking and its impact on military strategies and intelligence gathering.

Strategic planning and coordination are crucial elements of any military operation. Operation Mincemeat offers historians an opportunity to explore the strategic planning and coordination involved in executing a complex deception operation. By studying the decision-making processes and the collaboration between different branches of the military, historians can gain valuable insights into the strategic aspects of this operation.

The historical significance of Operation Mincemeat cannot be underestimated. It had a profound impact on the outcome of World War II. Historians can investigate the long-term implications of this operation, assessing how it shaped the course of the war and its subsequent impact on military strategies and intelligence operations.

Finally, Operation Mincemeat provides an intriguing case study for intelligence analysis. Historians can analyze the intelligence gathering, analysis, and interpretation process that led up to this operation. By examining the successes and failures of the intelligence community, historians can gain insights into the challenges and complexities of intelligence analysis during wartime.

Additionally, Operation Mincemeat highlights the use of propaganda and misinformation campaigns. Historians can study how these tactics were employed during this operation, exploring their implications and ethical implications. This subchapter offers a platform for deeper analysis of the role of propaganda and misinformation in wartime operations.

In conclusion, the implications for future historical investigations stemming from Operation Mincemeat are vast and multifaceted. From military history and espionage to psychological warfare and strategic planning, this subchapter provides a starting point for historians to explore the intricacies of this ingenious deception operation and its broader significance in the context of World War II.